AF548597

THE LOHF YEARS

THE LOHF YEARS

An Exhibition of Selected Rare Books and Manuscripts

Acquired by the Rare Book & Manuscript Library

While Kenneth A. Lohf Served as Its Librarian

1967–1992

COLUMBIA UNIVERSITY LIBRARIES

NEW YORK 1992

Catalogue compiled by Rudolph Ellenbogen

ISBN 0-9607862-4-4

With gratitude we dedicate this exhibition
to the donors over the past quarter of a century
whose gifts and support have strengthened
the Rare Book and Manuscript Library's
resources for study and research

FOREWORD by Elaine F. Sloan

Vice President for Information Services
and University Librarian

The decades since the close of World War II have been a time of impressive growth in the research resources of the Columbia University Libraries. Nowhere in our library system has this growth been more dynamic than in the collections of the Rare Book and Manuscript Library. As Librarian for Rare Books and Manuscripts for the past twenty-five years, Kenneth A. Lohf has overseen the remarkable development in its holdings. During those years the number of monographs doubled to a current total of one-half million volumes, and manuscripts increased from three million to twenty-six million individual items. During these same years the Rare Book and Manuscript Library acquired nearly 130,000 art works, paintings, drawings, prints, and photographs. The Library is truly a nationally important center for research in American and English literature and history, New York publishers and literary agents, history of economics and banking, performing arts, printing throughout the past five hundred years, history of mathematics and astronomy, and in virtually every other discipline in which study and research are carried on at this University.

These achievements and the beautifully renovated Rare Book and Manuscript Library are reflections of the singular success Ken has achieved through his work with the Friends of the Libraries and with other donors. The University is deeply indebted to him for his vision in forming a great collection and for his ability to enlist the support of others to make that vision a reality.

This catalogue documents the exhibition, "The Lohf Years," a selection of gifts of rare books and manuscripts received from 1967 to 1992, the period during which Ken served as Librarian for Rare Books and Manuscripts. It commemorates not only his own achievements as an institutional collector but also those benefactions of the more than 1,400 donors whose generosity has been the major component in the steady amassing of printed and manuscript treasures at the Library. The exhibition and its catalogue were organized by Rudolph S. Ellenbogen. They complement two other exhibitions held concurrently in Butler Library marking Ken's retirement at the end of this year after forty years of service at the Columbia Libraries. On the third floor of Butler, the focus is on his career; the exhibition includes a selection of his publications, a pictorial record of the building of the new Rare Book and Manuscript Library, and documents relating to his activities as Librarian, as President of The Grolier Club, and as a private collector. On the sixth floor, in the Rare Book and Manuscript Library itself, a display, entitled

"A Librarian's Gifts: A Selection of Books and Manuscripts Donated by Kenneth A. Lohf, 1958-1992," is also on view. The latter amply confirms Ken's commitment to the growth of collections and resources through private philanthropy, a tradition that he has sustained and nurtured throughout his Columbia career.

This catalogue and the exhibits document a truly remarkable career. We will miss Ken's daily presence but look forward to many years of continued support as a Friend of the Libraries.

INTRODUCTION by Dallas Pratt

The telephone rang in the University's Rare Book and Manuscript Library. "A call from President Kirk," the secretary said. It was the mid-1960s, and Kenneth Lohf wondered if there was any trouble as he picked up the phone. "Oh, Lohf," said Grayson Kirk in a perfectly calm voice, "I'm on to something which might interest you. Last night I dined with Bennett Cerf. He and his partner Donald Klopfer at Random House are looking for somewhere to bestow all their papers. He thought we might be interested. You might follow this up." All their papers! A house which had published W. H. Auden, William Faulkner, James Joyce, Sinclair Lewis, Eugene O'Neill, Gertrude Stein, and many other "greats" from the 1920s to the present day.

Ken followed up at once with a phone call to Random House. Nothing happened, however, immediately; in fact, nothing happened for four years. At last another telephone call, this time from Random House: "Will you come down and see what we have that's worth preserving?" Ken went down to their offices in the Villard mansion on Madison Avenue, was led through cavernous cellars and the boiler room by Bennett Cerf and Donald Klopfer, and emerged finally into a dark storeroom filled with scores of file cabinets arranged around the damp walls. The contents of several drawers were spilling onto the cement floor. How much was actually left in the files, the librarian wondered? Ken noticed the "St" file, walked over and opened it as a test, and there he feasted his eyes on a mass of Gertrude Stein folders containing hundreds of original letters and manuscripts and thousands of related items documenting her publishing career at Random House. The librarian felt both relieved and tremendously excited. Ken related this story to me at the beginning of my interview with him last summer.

"Acquiring this magnificent research resource for Columbia was one of the greatest thrills of my career as a librarian," said Ken. One of the treasures, a Eugene O'Neill manuscript of the introductions to his collected plays, is described under item 72. (Subsequent items mentioned in this introduction will be identified by the item number in parentheses). "What were some of the other 'thrills' in your quarter century as Columbia's Librarian for Rare Books and Manuscripts?" I asked, half-apologizing for associating thrills with the activities of Ken, a distinguished librarian, author of five full-length bibliographies, published poet, and formidable expert on manuscript and printed texts and on the book arts. "Oh, but there were lots of those in my career," he said. "Imagine being summoned to Tallahassee by Governor Reuben Askew of Florida to receive, at an open session of the state legislature, the contents of Cora Crane's safe deposit box which hadn't been opened since early in the century, and finding in it a wealth of documents relating both to Cora's and Stephen Crane's family, the pen with which Stephen wrote several of his novels, and Cora's riding-crop!"

With much pleasure and satisfaction Ken also recalled a more recent lunch at the Players' Club on Gramercy Park with Robert Giroux of Farrar, Straus and Giroux; as lunch was drawing to a close, his host said, "By the way, there's a shopping bag for you in the cloakroom as you leave," and in it Ken found the hefty manuscript, some six inches thick, of Thomas Merton's *The Seven Storey Mountain* (89) which Bob Giroux was presenting as a gift to the Merton Collection. The mention of Merton's name led me to ask, "I recall an outstanding Merton exhibition which you mounted in the Library in 1989. Was that mostly Columbia-owned?" "Oh, yes, we have a deeply felt commitment to Columbia authors, and of course Merton was among our most distinguished alumni. We were told by the Catholic chaplain at the University of the extensive collection of Merton manuscripts stored in the basement of the Notre Dame Church just a block from Butler Library. Since Father Merton had already written to me and had given a number of his manuscripts to the Library, we began negotiations posthaste that happily resulted in the large treasure trove being added to our Merton Collection."

Another group of Columbia authors whose books and manuscripts the Library acquired was the "Beats." "They all either went to Columbia College, as Allen Ginsberg (94) and Jack Kerouac (92) did, or lived in the Morningside Heights area," Ken explained. "The student riots in 1968 marked the genesis of the Library's interest in this group of Columbia authors. Ginsberg's poem, 'Howl,' was a student icon, and he was often on the campus to speak or give readings of his poems, and at one point he and Kerouac's biographer, Ann Charters, found my office on the eighth floor of Butler, high above the riot's turmoil, a convenient refuge for a meeting and interview. It was at one of these meetings that Allen and I began to talk about the depositing of his papers and library with us. For the sake of protection and future use of his literary archive, Allen readily agreed. Our brief talk and the rapid meeting of minds, seconded by Professors Barzun, Trilling, and Van Doren, resulted in the formation of the 'Beat' collection, now grown to be the most significant such literary archive of the movement in existence."

I was intrigued by the impressive and rapid growth in the collections and pursued that topic in our interview. "Ken, it seems you've been quite innovative in acquiring works in the realm of 'popular culture.' I note in the catalogue Paul R. Palmer's gift of a collection of 1,300 movie stills from the silent screen era to the present (76). Then, there is the manuscript and inscribed first edition of the first Ellery Queen novel, *The Roman Hat Mystery* (81), the gift of Richard and Douglas Dannay and Patricia Lee Caldwell. I saw these in a large exhibition of Columbia's mystery writer's material. Still another recent exhibition featured Nancy Saxon's gift of numerous delightful drawings by her late husband Charles for *New Yorker* covers and cartoons (101)." "Not only do these collections of popular culture mirror the social conventions of our age, but they also stimulate student interest," Ken explained. "But as an example of large attendance, certainly not confined to students nor related to popular culture, I should mention the exhibition held earlier this year, 'Jewish Literature Through the Ages,' drawn from a collection of more than one thousand manuscripts rarely exhibited but frequently used by scholars in our reading room." This exhibition is represented in the catalogue by a cuneiform tablet from the time of Abraham, which confirms the existence of some of the cities mentioned in the Book of Genesis (1). This important tablet was presented by Frances Henne, who was also the generous donor of over eight hundred children's books published in color by the McLoughlin Brothers in the nineteenth century (46).

"In the setting of the new Rare Book and Manuscript Library, opened in 1984," I noted, "the appearance of these exhibitions has created more interest and outshone all previous ones. How did this new construction come to pass?" It was obvious to all of us who had used the collections that the old quarters were cramped and could no longer accommodate the rapidly growing collections or the increasing number of students and researchers who were coming to use them. During Ken's tenure, the rare book collections have doubled in size to a half million volumes, and manuscript and archival collections have grown from three and one-half to twenty-six million items; there are also some 130,000 drawings, photographs, and memorabilia in the collections. Ken explained the process of building the new library: "The Rare Book and Manuscript Library was the last of Columbia's distinctive collections that needed modern premises to improve its operations, so I approached the University Librarian at that time, Patricia Battin, and received from her permission to draft a proposal for new quarters to present to the budget and space committees. She forwarded the proposal to them, and they approved and sent the proposal to the Board of Trustees, which also gave the project the green light with the proviso that we raise the necessary funds for the entire project." So, Ken began the mammoth task of raising the three million dollars needed to construct the new quarters from the truly inspired designs by Byron Bell, partner in the architectural firm of Cain, Farrell and Bell. Many Friends of the Libraries and other donors contributed generously, the Friends as a group specifically endowing the Donors Room, with fine period furnishings donated by the Viscountess Eccles. However, the major supporters were those after whom the other four units were named: Alan and Margaret Kempner, the exhibition room; Corliss Lamont, the rare book reading room; Mrs. George D. Woods, the manuscript reading room; and Ruth Ullman Samuel, the reference center.

On a visit to the new Library one is struck immediately by the spacious exhibition area, beautifully decorated in soft colors, the beamed and glass ceiling through which one can glimpse the sky, and the reading rooms with glass walls. I wondered what else one could wish for, and I asked Ken. "Oh, yes," he responded with a smile, "we do still need a great deal, especially a very necessary increase in the endowments of the Rare Book and Manuscript Library, and endowments as well for the positions of its librarians to secure the Library's future as a research center in a major university."

I then asked, "You've told me the story of your library and of some of its collections and their donors, but what about the librarian himself?" "To begin at the beginning," answered Ken, "I was a midwesterner, born in Milwaukee in 1925. As soon as I finished high school I was swept into the vortex of World War II: Officers Training Corps in the Air Force at Amherst and Yale, then overseas to Chittagong in India near the Burmese border as a first lieutenant. I was assigned to the instrument landing service, so vital because of our air supply routes over the Himalayas to western China. In this unlikely jungle setting with its monsoons and unbearable humidity and heat I started to write poetry, and after the war in the early 1950s my work began to appear in poetry magazines."

Ken's first book, a collection of thirty poems, *XXX for Time*, appeared in 1966, and five additional volumes, *Arrivals, Seasons, Fictions, Passages*, and *Places*, were published in the 1980s and 1990s. Demobilized from the Air Force in 1946, he enrolled in Northwestern University, majoring in English literature, and after graduating went to Columbia with the intention of becoming a college teacher. He earned his master's degree in 1950, with a thesis entitled "Graham Greene and the Problem of Evil." The first chapter of the thesis was published in a national magazine, the first of his writing to be printed.

"That sounds as though you were on the threshold of a literary career," I remarked. Ken responded, "Curiously enough, it proved more important in starting me on my way as a book collector. Since the library at that time was deficient in their holdings of Greene's books, I started to search the New York bookshops for his novels which were just becoming popular on this side of the Atlantic. For very little I acquired first editions of *Brighton Rock, England Made Me*, and *The Ministry of Fear*, among others. As for teaching, I eventually dropped the idea in favor of a library career because of my newly developed passion for identifying and gathering rare editions. I received a master's degree from the School of Library Service at Columbia in 1952, and then moved through several positions in the library system until I succeeded the late Roland Baughman as Librarian for Rare Books and Manuscripts in 1967–1968."

"Ken, since by your own admission you were 'hooked' as a book collector in your mid-twenties, it's not surprising that you're now known for several large and remarkable collections of your own," I remarked, "such as the art and literature of the Pre-Raphaelites and Victorian poetry, the writing of the English critic and poet Arthur Symons, and especially the work of the

British poets of the First and Second World Wars." "That's true, these are the areas on which I have concentrated as a collector, a sometimes costly and obsessive avocation, by the way. In my earliest serious collecting I concentrated on drawings, letters, and first editions of such figures as Burne-Jones, Holman Hunt, Rossetti, Landseer, and Ruskin. As to the First World War poets, I am particularly attracted by Rupert Brooke, Robert Graves, Siegfried Sassoon, and most of all, Wilfred Owen who ranks, I believe, not only as the supreme war poet but as among the finest English poets of all time. This collection includes some one hundred manuscripts and seven hundred first editions. From World War II I have more than one thousand first editions of British poets, and of these, Alun Lewis, who served in India as I did, appeals most to me."

I recalled to Ken two exhibitions which I had viewed at the Grolier Club in New York based on his collections—one on Sir Edward Burne-Jones in 1971 and another on the "Soldier Poets of the Great War" in 1988; they reminded me that Ken is currently president of the Grolier Club. He is also a fellow of the Pierpont Morgan Library and a council member of the American Museum in Britain. The last-named is a recent appointment, but the Council of the Friends of the Columbia Libraries has benefited from Ken's service as secretary-treasurer for the past twenty years. I, as editor of *Columbia Library Columns* until he and Rudolph Ellenbogen took over in 1981, greatly valued his assistance during the earlier years, including the lively and informative descriptions of gifts in his column, "Our Growing Collections," which for some twenty-five years has interested readers and pleased donors.

While Ken's service as secretary-treasurer provided the direction and continued growth of the organization and its programs, he reminisced with great pleasure about the Council officers and members with whom he was associated since the death in 1972 of Charles Mixer, who had served previously in that office. "The Friends have been fortunate in having the support of so many fine collectors and bibliophiles, and those who were the major forces in organizing the group in 1951, among them the Viscountess Eccles and yourself, Dallas, have done a great service to the Libraries in inspiring that support. Later notable officers of the Friends, among them Alan H. Kempner, Morris H. Saffron, Gordon N. Ray, and Frank Streeter have continued that tradition with distinction. In addition, donors have been especially generous in entrusting us with their family papers and their treasures, and many of these donors have over the years become my personal friends, such as Lita Hornick, George M. Jaffin, Corliss Lamont, Jack Harris Samuels, Iola Haverstick, and Louise Woods, among many, many others. All of them have enriched my professional and personal lives more fully than I can ever express."

I continued with my questions: "Ken, the Council of the Friends is continually astounded at their meetings by your reports of vast collections of papers and books which have been donated. Running through the catalogue, I note the Samuels Collection of two hundred volumes of seventeenth-century English drama (17); the Carnegie Corporation Papers (60); the Community Service Society Papers and the large group of early twentieth-century photographs (62); the Harper and Row contracts, including many for the publication of Herman Melville's novels (41); and the Simon & Schuster Papers, from which is selected Mrs. Schuster's gift of Beerbohm's drawing of G. B. Shaw lecturing to the Fabian Society (59). Added to these are the large collections of papers donated by literary agents, notably James Oliver Brown and Paul Revere Reynolds. We are talking about the addition of several hundred thousand items each year. How does your Library cope with these paper avalanches?" Ken, who is a prodigious worker himself, is always appreciative of the efforts of others, and he answered characteristically, "Because I have such a dedicated staff, headed by Bernard Crystal and Rudolph Ellenbogen, aided by their colleagues and a steady stream of student assistants, and with a little help from our friends the computers. Even though we are sometimes overwhelmed by the large gifts, they always remind us of the generosity of our thoughtful and loyal donors. Further, these gifts satisfy and encourage us because we know that students and scholars will make effective use of these resources in their studies and publications."

During his three and a half decades in the Rare Book and Manuscript Library, which he has headed for the past twenty-five years, Ken has directed much progress in constructing a new library, in building collections, and in encouraging research. The great original collections—Plimpton, Smith, Lodge, Brander Matthews, Seligman, Epstean, et al.—have been better cared for and more thoroughly used by several generations of Columbians and visiting scholars from across this country and from abroad. His encouragement for the establishment of endowed book purchase funds—such as the Solton and Julia Engel, Friends of the Libraries, Albert Ulmann, Louis and Marguerite Cohn, Herman and Aveve Cohen, and Jack Harris Samuels funds, to name those represented in the catalogue—has stimulated an ever-increasing inflow of gifts in cash and in kind, which amounted to $1.6 million last year.

Ken retires at the end of the year. He leaves behind a gift which is not mentioned in the catalogue yet may be the most valuable of all. Let me record it here: good will toward the Library, based on affection for Ken, of many hundreds of friends.

CATALOGUE

Incipit utilis tractatus cō-
fessionū editus p Reuerendū
frēz Antoninū archiepm̄. Flo.

D Efecerūt seru-
tantes scrutini-
o. Scrutiniuz
quoddā ē cōfes-
in quo & penitēs scrutatur
consciāz suā. & cōfessor cū eo.
Scrutans ergo ē cōfessor q ī hoc
pōt tripl'r deficē. ¶ Quia
uel p malitiaz absoluēdo quē
scit nō posse. ¶ Vel p igno-
rantiā nesciens discernē in-
ter leprā & quē possit uel
nō possit absoluē ul' per in-
firmitatē cōcupiscētie. inde
sumens occasiones malorum ex
auditu dū ī caute se habet.
Vnde aug' de pe. di. vj. c. j.
¶ Caueat spūalis iudex
ut sicut non cōmisit crimē
nequitie: ita nō careat mu-
nē sciē. Ex qbus innuit ubiq
qd debz hrē potatē ī foro con-
sciē ut sit iudex spūalis.
et cōseruare puritatem uite
ne cōmittat crimen neqtie
et scientie sufficientē clari-
tatem habere. ut non ca-
reat munere scientie. ¶
De potestate seu auctē cō-
fessionis & qs possit audire cōfe.

V Bi notandū est qd non
sacerdos & si possit audire in casu mortis. nō tn̄ absol-
uere. alias si absoluit ut sacerdos indicatiue secundū qsdaz
incurrit irregl'aritatē. sicut si
celebraret. hoc tn̄ ē dubiū qa
nō est istud expressū ī iure
sicut de celebrāte. vn̄ non
uidetur irregl'aritas. ex de sen.
excō. li. vj. is. & talis cōfessus
tenetur iterum cōfiteri. rō ē. quia
solis sacerdotib' dēm ē. quorum
remiseritis pcc̄a remittuntur. Jo. xx.
¶ Nec tn̄ a quolibet sacerdote
pōt qs absolui sed a proprio
aut de licentia eius. Unde decre-
talis in ca. Oīs utriusq. ex de
pe. & re. dicit q. qlibet semel
confiteatur oīa pcc̄a sua propo
sacerdoti. & de pe. & re. di. vj.
ca. placuit. rō est. qa nō pōt
absoluē ul ligarē nisi hēat iu-
risdictionēz sup eū q sibi cō-
fitetur. ¶ Si aūt sit pprius pre-
latus & nō sacēdos. sicut electi
& epi nō sacerdotes. possunt
absoluē p aliū cōmittens hoc
alteri. ¶ Sed nō qd proprius
sacēdos aliter ītelligitur cuz
dicitur qd qlibet debet cōfi-

1. Cuneiform tablet, ca. 2060 B.C. 11 cm. high.

Found in southern Babylonia in the vicinity of Ur of the Chaldees, the birthplace of Abraham, the cone is of interest because it confirms the existence of some of the cities mentioned in the Book of Genesis. The inscription is among the best examples yet discovered of writing contemporaneous with Abraham and from his own country.

GIFT OF FRANCES HENNE, 1973

2. Walter Map, fl. 1200. La mort Artu. Manuscript on vellum and paper, 94 leaves. Northern France, 14th century.

Pen work initials in red and blue through the first thirty-two leaves. From the collection of Howard Lehman Goodhart with his bookplate, the manuscript contains the fifth and last part of the Walter Map Arthurian cycle.

BEQUEST OF ROGER SHERMAN LOOMIS (LITT.D., 1957), 1966

3. St. Antoninus, 1389–1459. Tractatus confessorum. Manuscript on vellum, 132 leaves. Italy, 1472.

An excerpt of the author's *Summa theologica moralis*. Written in a clear semi-gothic hand, with nine finely painted and illuminated initials and many ornamental letters; bound in a contemporary Venetian binding, leather on oak boards with blind stamped ornaments; from the celebrated collection of the Reverend Walter Sneyd.

GIFT OF MR. AND MRS. ROBERT CREMIN, 1973

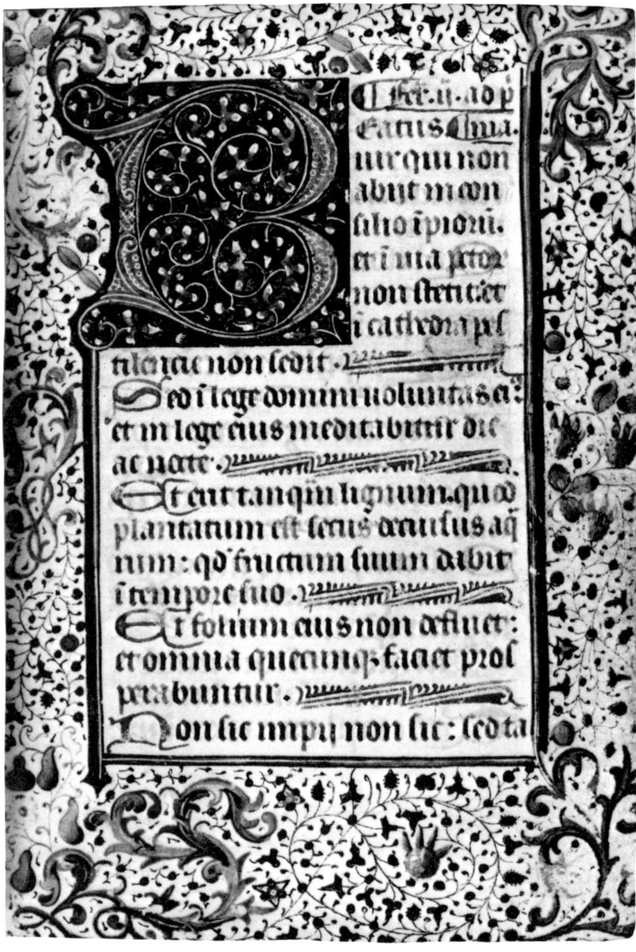

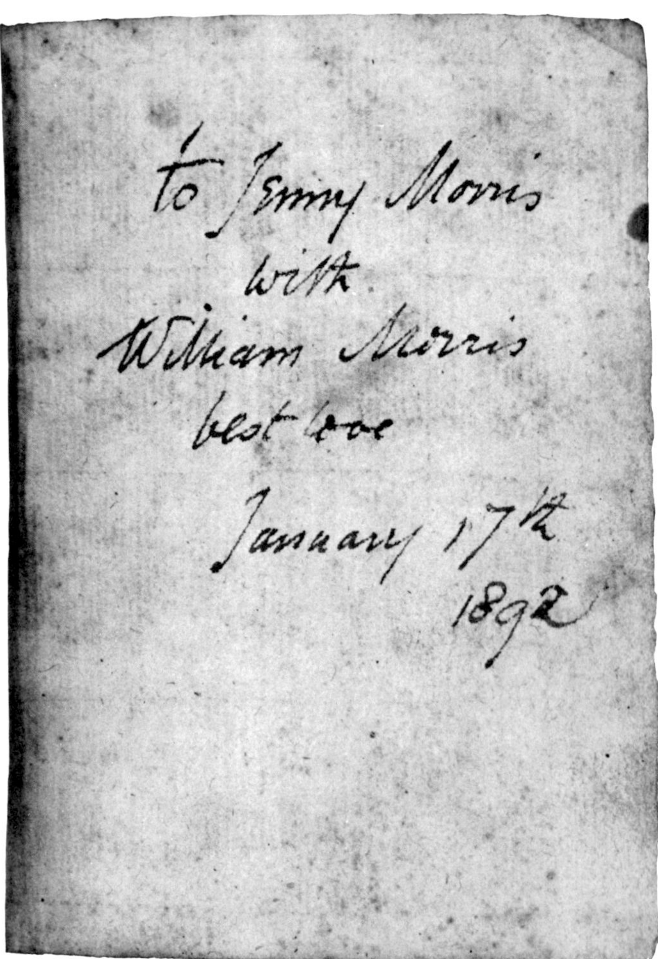

4

4. Psalms, followed by the Canticles and Litany of Saints, preceded by a Calendar for a Celestine convent. Manuscript on vellum, 196 leaves. France, late 15th century.

Decorated throughout with red and blue initials and illuminated with seventeen larger gold embossed letters within floral borders; bound in contemporary calf with brass clasps. Inscribed by William Morris to his eldest daughter, Jenny (Jane Alice Morris), January 17, 1892.

GIFT OF MARGARET L. KEMPNER IN MEMORY OF ALAN H. KEMPNER (A.B. 1917), 1986

5. Book of Revelations. Mainz: [Johann Gutenberg and Johann Fust, ca. 1454–1455].

The first printing of the last book of the New Testament from the "Gutenberg Bible." From the library of A. Edward Newton with his note and bookplate and with a bibliographical essay by Newton printed under the direction of Bruce Rogers in 1921.

GIFT OF THE MARY FLAGLER CARY CHARITABLE TRUST, 1968

6. Matthaeus de Cracovia, ca. 1335–1420. *Dialogus rationis et conscientiae de frequenti usu communionis.* [Mainz: 1460].

Rubricated and decorated throughout, the volume, containing an additional five fifteenth-century religious works, is bound in contemporary calf over beech wood boards. The Matthaeus de Cracovia is one of the few books issued by "the Printer of the *Catholicon*," who has frequently been identified as Johann Gutenberg.

GIFT OF THE MARY FLAGLER CARY CHARITABLE TRUST, 1969

Vniuerſis preſentes inſpecturis ĩnoteſcat q̄
poſuit ĩ capſa in eccleſia cõuentus fratrũ heremitarũ ordinis ſcĩ Auguſtini obſeruãtie Creme
elemoſinã ꝓut eius deuotio dictauit. Et ideo ex auctoritate apoſtolica facultatẽ hꝫ ꝓut patet
ex Bulla plũbea ſciſſimi dñi nr̃i Innocẽtii pape octaui. q̄ eſt ĩ p̄dicto Cõuentu eligẽdi ꝯfeſſo
re idoneũ preſbiterũ ſecularẽ uel cuiuſuis etiã mẽdicantiũ ordinis regularẽ. Qui eius cõfeſſione diligẽter
audita ꝓ ꝯmiſſis exceſſibus ⁊ peccatis ac cẽſuris eccleſiaſticis qbuſlibet ẽt ĩ ſingulis ſedi apoſtolice reſer
uatis caſibus ſ. uel ĩ vita. ⁊ in nõ reſeruatis totiens quotiẽs opus fuerit abſoluere ⁊ ĩ mortis articulo ter
tie partis peccatorũ remiſſionem ĩpendere. ac emiſſa p̄ eum vota quecunqꝫ. vltramarino. viſitatiõis limi
nũ apoſtolorũ Petri ⁊ Pauli ac eccleſie ſcĩ Jacobi in compoſtella necnõ ingreſſus religionis ⁊ caſtitatis
votis dũtaxat exceptis in alia pietatis opa valeat cõmutare. Et in fidem premiſſorum. Ego frater Augu
ſtinus de Crema prior p̄dicti conuentus manu propria me ſubſcripſi ⁊ ſigillo ad hoc deputato ĩpreſſio
ne muniui.

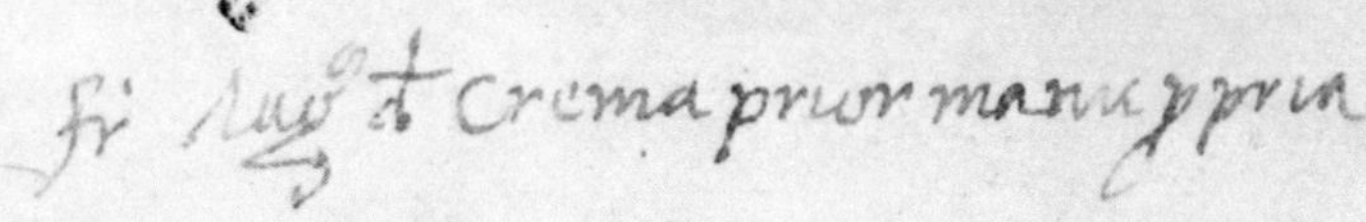

7. Pope Innocent VIII, 1432–1492. Lettera indulgentiae. [Milan: Leonard Pachel, between 1484 and 1492].

A unique and unrecorded Italian incunable broadside containing the text of an indulgence, issued by Pope Innocent VIII in favor of a newly founded monastery of the Augustinian Hermits in Crema, and signed by Augustinus de Crema, the abbot.

GIFT OF MR. AND MRS. WILLIAM SALLOCH, 1983

8. Stephan Fridolin (Pater Stephan), 1430–ca. 1498. *Schatzbehalter der wahren Reichtümer des Heils.* Nuremberg: Anton Koberger, 1491.

The first and only edition of one of the monuments of German fifteenth-century wood engraving and printing, the ninety-six colored woodcut illustrations by Michael Wolgemut (the master of Dürer), 1434–1519, are considered the artist's finest achievement. The illustrations in this copy are hand colored by a contemporary artist. Bound in pigskin over wooden boards, stamped in blind in panel design, with eagles in four corners within diamonds.

GIFT OF THE MARY FLAGLER CARY CHARITABLE TRUST, 1970

9. ʻAbd al-Raḥmān ibn ʻUmar ibn Sūfī, 903–986. *Kitāb suwar al-kawākib* (Book of pictures of the fixed stars). Persian manuscript translated from the Arabic, 127 leaves. 16th century.

One of the three masterpieces of Muslim observational astronomy by one of the greatest Muslim astronomers, known in only eight copies. This manuscript contains seventy-four miniatures of the constellation figures painted in color and has been used as a model book for the transfer of illustrations to other manuscripts.

PURCHASED WITH FUNDS DONATED BY THE HAGOP KEVORKIAN FOUNDATION, 1968

10. Pope Leo X, 1475–1521. Bull directed to the Abbey of Saint Bertim in the Diocese of Thérouanne. Manuscript on vellum, with lead seal and silk cord. Rome, 1519.

For 12,000 ducats the Abbey was granted exemption from the jurisdiction of the local bishop and was permitted to perform certain functions otherwise allowed only to the bishop, such as granting special indulgences or dedicating churches, and was given spritual jurisdiction over all mendicants. One year later a bull from Leo to Martin Luther was burned, marking the beginning of Protestantism.

GIFT OF MR. AND MRS. ROBERT CREMIN, 1970

11. Francisco Pizarro, 1475–1541. Document granting power of attorney to Bernardino de San Pedro to collect 628 gold pesos. [1538?].

Signed by the conquistador within his characteristic double paraph.

GIFT OF DANIEL DEL RIO, 1967

12. Playing cards. France, Italy, and Germany: 15th and 16th centuries.

An album of sixty-eight playing cards, including portions of four separate sets of German and Italian woodcuts and a single woodcut, possibly French, the Knave of Swords, retouched with gray wash.

GIFT OF JOHN F. FLEMING, 1981

13. John Gower, ca. 1330–1408. *De confessione amantis*. London: Thomas Berthelette, 1554.

Third edition of one of the classics of Middle English. The George Daniel, Mark Masterman Sykes, Robert Hoe, Beverly Chew copy. Bound by Roger Payne.

GIFT OF MR. AND MRS. HAL HIGGINBOTHAM (M.S., 1969, D.L.S., 1985), 1985

14. Evangelary. Latin manuscript on vellum of the Four Gospels, 94 leaves. Spain, probably Barcelona, between 1577 and 1588.

Written by a master calligrapher of the Renaissance in Roman letters, with numerous illuminated initials in gold and colors, several historiated in a baroque manner. The first leaf is illuminated in gold on a crimson background with a full border of flowers and fruit on a ground of liquid gold.

GIFT OF JOHN M. CRAWFORD, JR., 1971

15. Laurence Johnson, fl. 1570–1578. *Cometographia quaedam lampadis aeriae que 10 die Nouemb. apparuit, anno a Vigineo partu. 1577.* London: Robert Walley, 1578.

Issued under the pseudonym, L. Bariona, the work on the comet of 1577 is one of three known copies.

GIFT OF MORTON PEPPER IN MEMORY OF C. DORIS HELLMAN (PH.D., 1933), 1975

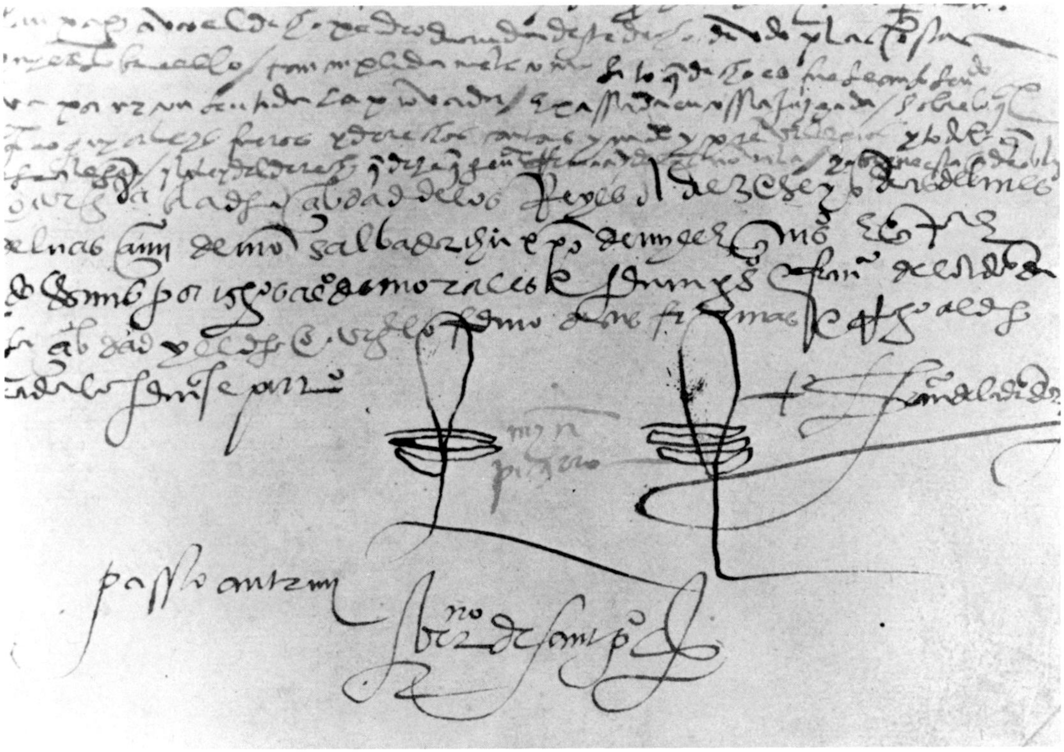

11

12

¶ COMETOGRAPHIA quædam Lampadis aeriæ quę 10. die Nouemb. apparuit, Anno a *Virgineo partu*. 1577.

Iris vt est signum, terras perijsse sub vndis:
Ignibus est ignis cuncta casura suis.

Londini excudebat Robertus Walley.
Anno Domini, 1578.

16. Sir Francis Bacon, 1561–1626. Letter book of state papers. Manuscript, 95 p. [England, ca. 1630].

Twenty-six letters by Bacon and twenty by others, copies in three scribal hands. The letters by Bacon, including some of his most notable, date from 1595 to 1621, and are addressed to James I, Robert Cecil, Lords Northumberland and Southampton, Sir Thomas Egerton, among many others. There are also letters from Sir Thomas Bodley, founder of the Bodleian Library in Oxford, to Bacon; a letter from the imprisoned Duke of Norfolk to Queen Elizabeth in 1571; and letters relating to the abortive negotiations for the Spanish marriage of Prince Charles in 1623.

PURCHASED ON THE JACK HARRIS SAMUELS (A.M., 1940) FUND, 1988

17. Christopher Marlowe, 1564–1593. *The famous tragedy of the rich jew of Malta*. London: Printed by J. Beale for Nicholas Vavasour, 1633.

First edition of the rarest of the nearly two hundred quarto editions in the Samuels collection of English drama from the Elizabethan and Restoration periods.

BEQUEST OF MOLLIE HARRIS SAMUELS FROM THE LIBRARY OF JACK HARRIS SAMUELS (A.M., 1940), 1974

18. *Book of Common Prayer*. London: Robert Barker, and by the assignes of John Bill, 1638.

The Shelley family Bible, with the signature of Sir Timothy Shelley, Percy Bysshe Shelley's father, on the title page; on the page facing are the names of John and Mary Shelley, Sir Timothy's uncle and aunt, and Hellen Shelley, John Shelley's aunt. Also bound in the volume are the *Holy Bible*, 1639, *Concordance, or table to the Bible*, 1639, and *Whole Book of Psalms*, 1638.

GIFT OF ALAN H. KEMPNER (A.B., 1917), 1984

19. "Lawes Establish't by the Authority of his Majesties Letters Patents graunted to His Royall Highness James Duke of Yorke and Albany . . . Publish't . . . by virtue of a Commission . . . Bearing date the second day of Aprill 1664." Manuscript, 132 p., with additions, 52 p., 1664–1677.

Signed by Richard Nicolls, the first English governor of New York, Francis Lovelace, second governor, and Matthias Nicolls, secretary of the province. Covering a wide range of subjects, the eighty "Dukes Laws" were compiled after the conquest of New Amsterdam by the Duke of York. This copy, one of four known copies, had been in the Van Cortlandt family since the eighteenth century.

GIFT OF MRS. CHARLES BLYTH (VAN CORTLANDT) MARTIN, 1978

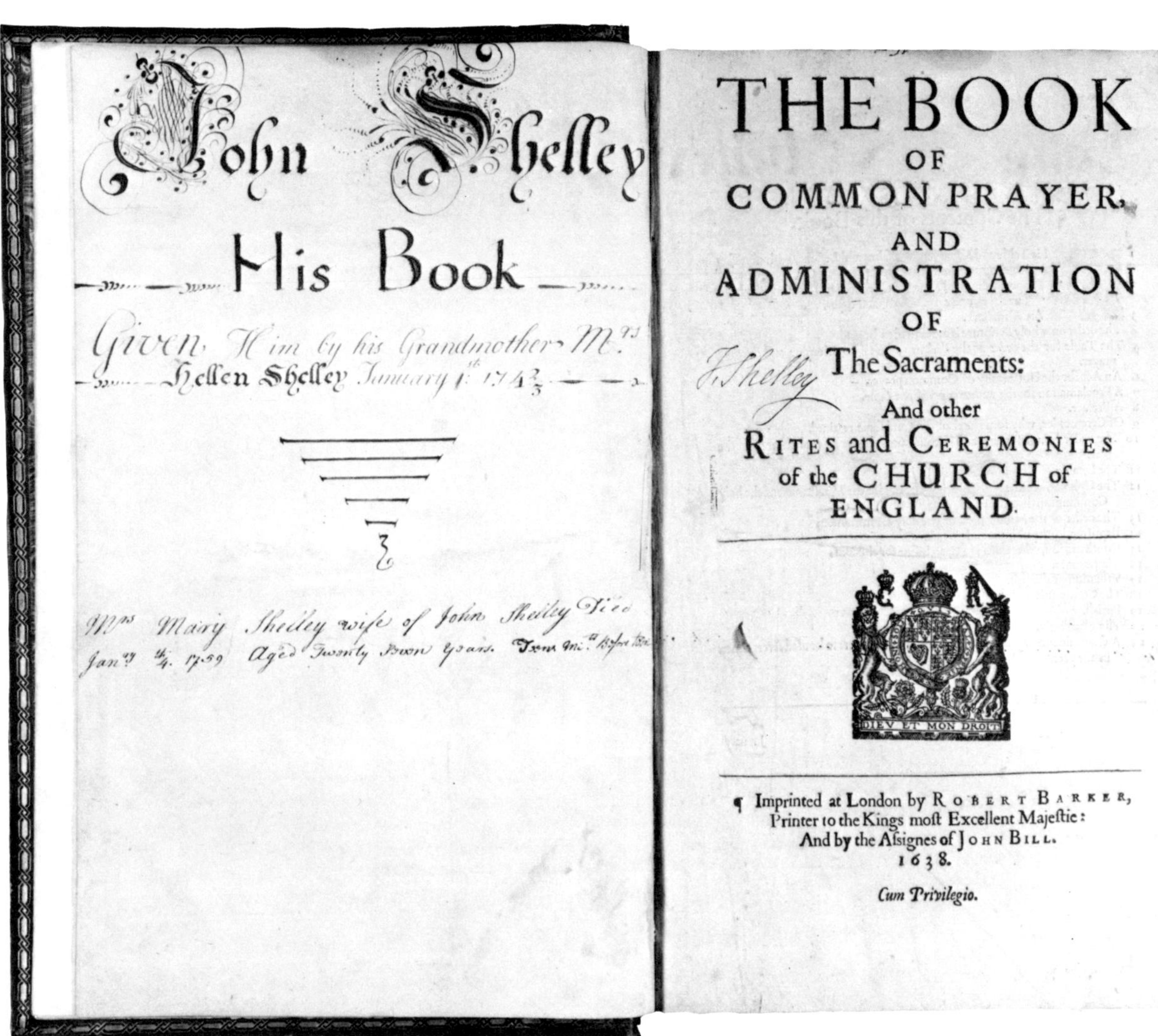

John Shelley
His Book
Given Him by his Grandmother Mrs
Hellen Shelley January 1st 1742/3

Mrs Mary Shelley wife of John Shelley Died
Jan.ry 4. 1759 Aged Twenty Seven Years.

THE BOOK
OF
COMMON PRAYER.
AND
ADMINISTRATION
OF
The Sacraments:
And other
RITES and CEREMONIES
of the CHURCH of
ENGLAND.

DIEU ET MON DROIT

¶ Imprinted at London by ROBERT BARKER,
Printer to the Kings most Excellent Majestie:
And by the Assignes of JOHN BILL.
1638.

Cum Privilegio.

18

[r]edresse for In-
[ju]ryes done to
[I]ndyans.

All Injuryes done to the Indyans, of what
nature soeuer shall upon their complaint, and
proofe thereof in any Court, haue speedy redresse
gratis, against any Christian, in as full and
ample manner (with reasonable allowance of
damage) as if the Case had beene betwixt a
Christian and Christian.

19

20. Sir Isaac Newton, 1642–1727. The three mysterious fires: commentary on Johann de Monte-Snyder's *Tractus de medicina universali....* After 1678. Autograph manuscript, 3p., in English and Latin.

Newton devoted many years of his life to the study of chemistry, alchemy, and metallurgy, and the depth of his interest in these subjects is demonstrated by this manuscript.

GIFT OF THE FRIENDS OF THE COLUMBIA LIBRARIES, 1971

21. Longus. *Les amours pastorals de Daphnis et Chloé.* [Paris: Quillau], 1718.

From the library of Horace Walpole with his bookplate and signed autograph note, "This is the genuine edition and very scarce. The cuts were designed by the Regent of France, Philip Duke of Orleans. This copy was purchased at the sale of Vice-Chamberlain Coke, by Maria Skerrett, afterwards, second wife of my father, Sir Robert Walpole, First Earl of Orford H. W."

GIFT OF MESSRS. ADRIAN P. AND DAVID E. MOORE FROM THE ESTATE OF EDITH PULITZER MOORE, 1975

22. John Martyn, 1699–1768. "To the Author of the Grubstreet Journal." Autograph manuscript, 82 p. [London?], 6 September 1731/2.

The Grub-Street Journal, edited by Martyn and Richard Russel, was a weekly paper issued from 1730 to 1737 which satirized contemporary issues and literary works such as Richard Bentley's edition of *Paradise Lost.* Some of the attacks on Bentley's edition, in the form of letters, are signed "Zoilus," a pseudonym frequently used by Martyn. This manuscript, most likely in the hand of Martyn, is a compendium of these letters.

GIFT OF MORRIS SAFFRON (A.B. 1925,: A.M., 1949; PH.D., 1968), 1987

23. Alexander Pope, 1688–1744. Oil painting on copper after Jean Baptist Van Loo (1684–1745). ca. 1740? 29 x 22 cm.

This is one of two eighteenth-century oil portraits of Pope, the other by George Lumley (1708?–1768), in the Halsband Collection.

GIFT OF ROBERT HALSBAND (A.M.,1936), 1984

24. New York (City) Mayor's Court. Ledger of court fees and cases. Manuscript, 249 p. New York, 1758–1776.

Kept by Augustus Van Cortlandt (1728–1823), a court clerk, the manuscript includes entries for prominent New Yorkers, John Jay, Egbert Benson, Philip Livingston, Robert R. Livingston, Peter Van Schaack, and Richard Varick, among others.

GIFT OF KATHERINE VAN CORTLANDT WILBERDING, 1979

25. *A plan of the boundary lines betweeen the Province of Maryland and the three lower counties on Delaware with part of the parallel of latitude which is the boundary between the provinces of Maryland and Pennsylvania.* [Philadelphia: Robert Kennedy, 1768]. 2 sheets, 54.5 x 76 cm., 54.5 x 77 cm.

The surveyors Charles Mason and Jeremiah Dixon established the boundary line in 1767, which was to bear their names, resolving a dispute of nearly ninety years between the Penns and the Baltimores. The boundary, 244 miles in length, is printed on two sheets, the eastern line on a single copperplate, the western line, because of its length, divided into three parts, one engraved under the other. This copy belonged to Benjamin Chew (1722–1810), a member of the Boundary Commission established in 1750 by the English High Court.

GIFT OF THE CHEW FAMILY THROUGH THE COURTESY OF JOHN T. CHEW, 1983

25

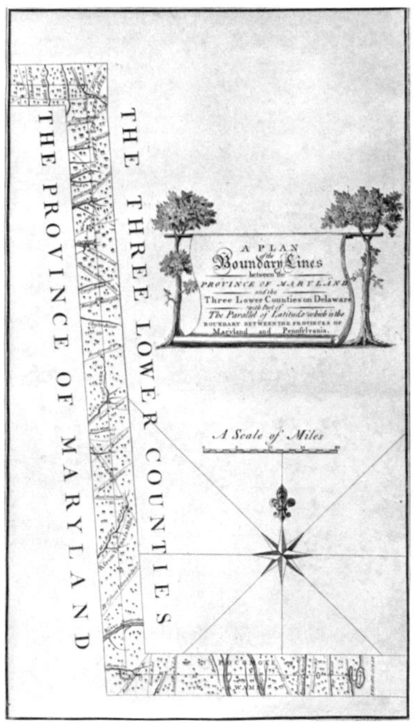

that he recd. this Information from the Englishman's own Mouth —

Mr Oswald spoke handsomely of Mr Poultney's Caracter — I advised him to trace the Matter further, and if true, to get it properly authenticated, which he promised to do —

24 Octr. Mr Oswald told me he had recd. a Courier last Night — that our articles were under Consideration, & that Mr Strachey, Ld Towsend's Secy was on the way here to confer with us abt. them.

Mr Oswald declined informing me of the particular Objections, but it was easy to perceive from his Conversation that they related to the back Lands, & he further said "he believed this Court had found Means to put a Spoke in our Wheel: — he told me that Fitzherbert had recd. an answer to the french Propositions, that this answer inadvertently gave away the Gum Trade, and that he had in vain desired him to postpone the Delivery of the answer till he should apprize his Court of the Mistake, and give them an opportunity of correcting it — He consulted me on the possibility of keeping Mr Stracheys coming a Secret — I told him it was not possible, and that it wd. be best to declare the Truth abt. it. viz that he was coming with Books & Papers relative to our Boundaries

He also mentioned to me his having recd. several Letters from a Gentlen. at St. Germains inviting him to go there & promising to communicate something of great Importance — he shewed me the last Letter — I advised him to go, especially as the Gent. seemed to press it exceedingly.

Dined with Dr. Franklin — I found Mr De Rayneval there — just ~~before~~ after Dinner, the Dr. informed me that Raynevalle had sent him word that he wd. dine with him to Day & wd be glad to meet me there — I told the Dr. what I had heard from Oswald abt. Strachey, & that I thought it best

26. George Washington, 1732–1799. Memorandum survey book. Autograph manuscript, 11 p. [Virginia] 10–14 March 1769.

In this manuscript, Washington recorded his survey of the land in northwest Virginia that he purchased from the estate of George Carter.

GIFT OF MRS. FRANCIS T. P. PLIMPTON, 1987

27. John Jay, 1745–1829. Diary kept during the peace negotiations. Manuscript, 10 p. Paris, 23 June–22 December 1782.

Jay, who served with Benjamin Franklin and John Adams as one of the American commissioners in the negotiations with Great Britain, kept this diary in which he recorded significant events relating to the peace negotiations which culminated in the Treaty of Paris, 1783, ending the American Revolution.

GIFT OF THE CLASS OF 1923 IN MEMORY OF GÉRARD TONACHEL, 1973

28. Phillis Wheatley, 1753?–1784. *Poems on various subjects, religious and moral.* London: Printed; Philadelphia: Re-printed, and sold by Joseph Crukshank, 1786.

First American editon of the first book of poems by an African-American and the first substantial work by an African-American to be published in this country. Although the English edition is common, there are only seven known copies of the American edition.

PURCHASED ON THE CHARLES W. MIXER (B.S., 1934) FUND, 1983

29. Henry Essex Edgeworth de Firmont, Abbé Edgeworth, 1745–1807. Autograph letter, signed, to Mrs. D. Tunstall. [Choisy-le-Roi, France] 18 February [1793].

Written less than a month after the execution of Louis XVI by the Irish clergyman who accompanied the king to the scaffold and assisted him as priest during the execution, this letter describes the King's final moving words and fateful moments, as well as the effect of his death on the Abbé's own circumstances.

GIFT OF DALLAS PRATT (M.D., 1941), 1984

Compleating the Regiments and altering the establishm.t of them.

The necessity of the first, in the most expeditious manner possible, is too self evident, to need arguments to prove; and therefore I shall only beg leave to recommend the mode, as voluntary enlistments seem to be totally out of the question, and drafting for the War, or three years will be disgusting and dangerous. I would beg leave to propose an annual draft of Militia without officers to serve till the first day of January in each year, that on or before the first day of October preceeding, these drafted men should be called upon to reinlist for the succeeding year—and, as an inducement to them to do so (as they would be much better, and less expensive than raw recruits) a bounty of 25 Dollars be offered them—that, upon ascertaining at this period the number of Men willing to reinlist, exact returns shall be made to Congress of the deficiency of each Regiment and transmitted by them to the States they belong with a request to have their respective quotas immediately furnished and sent on to Camp for the service of the ensuing year to be there before the

30

30. George Washington, 1732–1799. Proposals for the new American army after the revolution. Autograph manuscript, 4 p. 1798 or 1799.

Draft of the president's proposals with numerous revisions, the manuscript has sections headed "Half-pay, & Pensionary establishment" and "Compleating the Regiments and altering the establishm. of them."

GIFT OF MARIE HAMILTON McDAVID BARRETT, 1988

Geo Town —
2. Sep. 1814.

My Dr Father. —

It was with great pleasure we heard from you that you were all well - it had been so long since we had any news of you. - Polly goes up in the morning with Chs Lowe - I cannot go yet, as I have to make a journey to the Fleet to try to get Dr Beanes released from the Enemy. - I hope I may succeed but I think it very doubtful. When I return I shall get to the Dists as soon as possible. — I fear it will be quite impossible to get a loan as you mention from the Banks neither the Banks here, nor in Fredk (as I understand) make any discounts. - I owe more money in Bank here now than I ought - & in these distressing times I really know not what I shall do to provide for the necessities of my family. - I think you had better sell something even at a sacrifice to raise what you want, & then avoid incurring, on any account, any new debt. - Your [illegible] what I would certainly advise you to sell, if you can get any thing, even 75 cents for it. It cannot be more saleable - There is no hope of peace and as the war lasts that & every thing else will be getting worse. — In about a fortnight I trust I shall see you - sooner if I can - Farewell my dr Father - yr most affecte son

FSK

The Enemy have left Alexa to-day. - Tell the children I would write to them but have not time.

31

31. Francis Scott Key, 1799–1843. Autograph letter, signed, to John Ross Key. George Town, 2 September 1814.

In this letter, Key writes to his father about the mission to release a physician captured by the British; it is the earliest known account of the occasion that led to the writing of "The Star-Spangled Banner."

GIFT OF MR. AND MRS. ALFRED C. BEROL, 1972

32. Don José Fernando de Abascal y Sousa, 1743–1821, and Don Joaquín de la Pezuela y Sanchez Muñoz de Velasco, 1761–1830. Manuscript documents, signed by the viceroys and other officials. 241 leaves. Peru, 1815–1816.

The approximately 325 manuscript documents, bound in two volumes, represent the activities of the last two Spanish viceroys in Peru during the period immediately preceding the revolution and the founding of the modern state of Peru.

GIFT OF FLORENCE FINELLI IN MEMORY OF RAY TRAUTMAN (B.S., 1940), 1982

MEMORANDUMS, OBSERVATIONS, AND APPOINTMENTS,
In June, 1816.

33. Hester Lynch Thrale Piozzi, 1741–1821. Diary. Autograph manuscript, signed, 112 p., 15 p. 1816.

Mrs. Piozzi recorded her activities, her health, the weather, and the life at Bath in this daily diary, one of four in the collection of Professor James L. Clifford.

GIFT OF JAMES L. CLIFFORD (A.M., 1932; PH.D., 1941) AND VIRGINIA CLIFFORD, 1978

34. Mary Wollstonecraft (Godwin) Shelley, 1797–1851. *Frankenstein, or, the modern Prometheus.* London: Lackington, Hughes, Harding, Mavor & Jones, 1818. 3 volumes.

First edition, in the original boards.

BEQUEST OF MOLLIE HARRIS SAMUELS FROM THE LIBRARY OF JACK HARRIS SAMUELS (A.M., 1940), 1974

35

13
Who is this that darkeneth counsel by words without knowledge
Then the Lord answered Job out of the Whirlwind
Who maketh the Clouds his Chariot & walketh on the Wings of the Wind
Hath the Rain
a Father & who hath begotten
the Drops of the Dew
W Blake invenit & sculp
London Published as the Act directs March 8: 1825 by William Blake N 3 Fountain Court Strand
Proof

36

35. Gilbert Stuart Newton, 1794–1832. Sir Walter Scott. Oil on artists board. 22.5 x 18.5.

Inscribed on verso of the portrait, "Painted by G. S. Newton at Abbotsford in 1824 as vivam."

GIFT OF SAM AND KATALIN SCHAEFLER, 1984

36. William Blake, 1757–1827. *Illustrations of the Book of Job*. London: William Blake, 1825.

Eighteen proof sets on India paper with the incorrect date, 1828, on the first plate were issued; this set is from the library of John Addington Symonds and contains his bookplate.

PURCHASED ON THE SOLTON (A.B., 1916) AND JULIA ENGEL FUND, 1965

37. Octavia Walton LeVert, 1810–1877. Autograph album, 180 p. 1827–1830.

Octavia Walton, daughter of the first civilian governor of Florida, was visiting Baltimore on May 1, 1827, at which time Edgar Allan Poe inscribed a nine-line poem beginning, "When wit, and wine, and friends have met," in her album. Other notable inscriptions are by Henry Clay, Thomas Moore, the Irish poet, and Edward Coote Pinkney, the southern poet.

PURCHASED ON VARIOUS FUNDS, 1968

38. Benjamin Disraeli, 1804–1881. *The young duke*. London: Henry Colburn and Richard Bentley, 1831. 3 volumes.

Disraeli's second novel; inscribed by the author to Mrs. Sarah Austen, a close friend, who was instrumental in arranging for the publication of Disraeli's first novel.

GIFT OF WILLIAM B. LIEBMANN, 1979

39. Nicholas Harris Nicolas, 1799–1848. *History of the orders of knighthood of the British Empire of the Order of Guelphs of Hanover, and of the medals, clasps, and crosses conferred for naval and military services*. London: J. Hunter, 1842. 4 volumes.

Illustrations by George Baxter; printed by Charles Whittingham. The magnificent double-spread title page in color has been called one of the finest title page openings of the century.

GIFT OF MR. AND MRS. T. PETER KRAUS, 1984

40. Clement Clarke Moore, 1779–1863. *A visit from St. Nicholas.* New York: Henry Onderdonk, 1848.

One of the few known copies of the first separate publication in booklet form of "The night before Christmas." The text was first published in the *Troy Sentinel* in 1823 and in book form in Moore's *Poems* in 1844.

GIFT OF THE MARY FLAGLER CARY CHARITABLE TRUST, 1970

41. Contract between Herman Melville, 1819–1891, and Harper and Brothers for "The whale" [i.e., Moby Dick]. Manuscript, 2 p., signed by Allan Melville for Herman Melville. New York, 12 September 1851.

The Harper and Brothers collection also contains contracts for Melville's *Mardi*, *Omoo*, *Pierre*, *Redburn*, *Typee*, and *White-jacket*. *Omoo*, *Mardi*, and *Typee* are signed by Melville; the others are signed by his brother Allan Melville.

GIFT OF HARPER & ROW, 1975 AND 1989

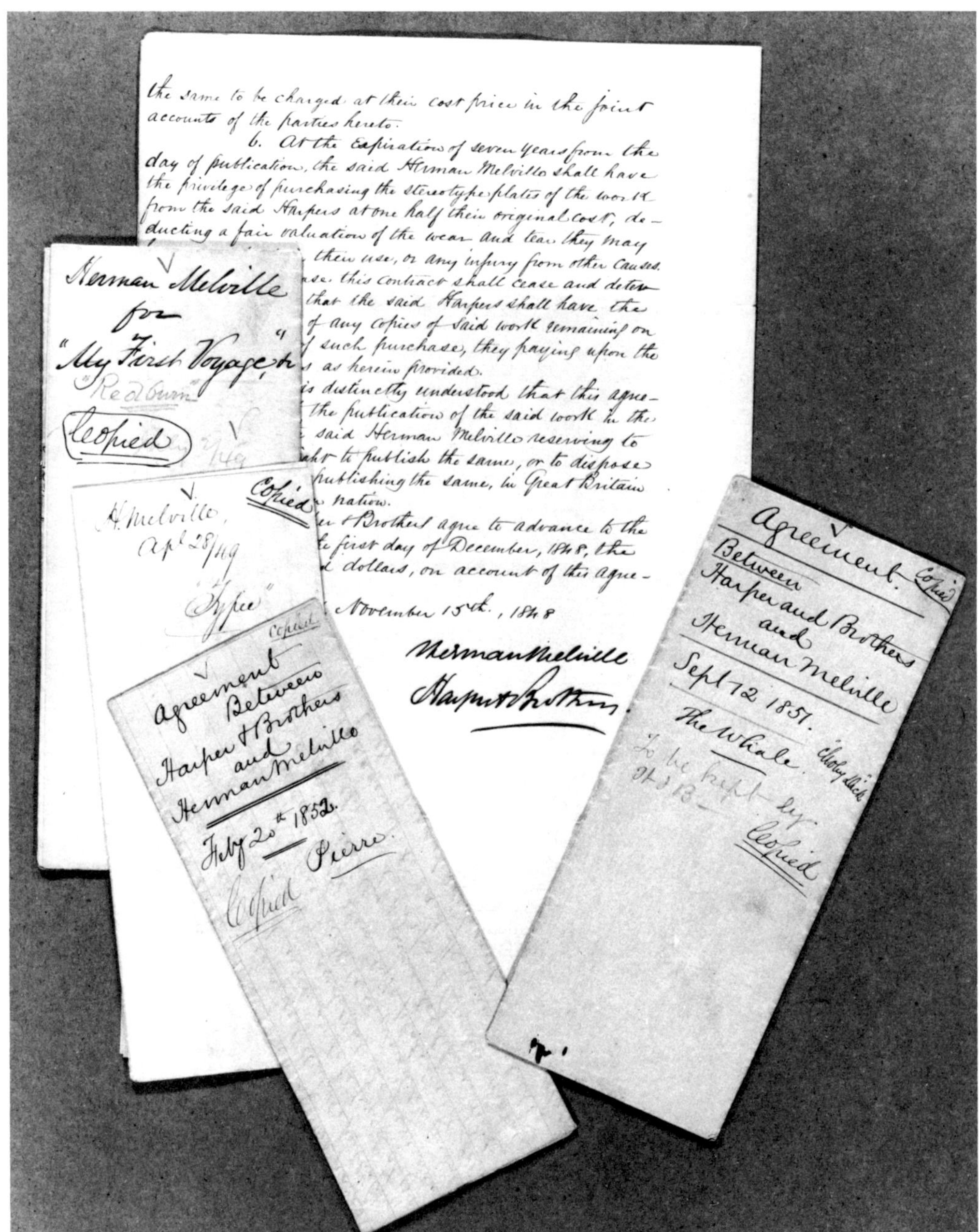
the same to be charged at their cost price in the joint
accounts of the parties hereto.
6. At the expiration of seven years from the
day of publication, the said Herman Melville shall have
the privilege of purchasing the stereotype plates of the work
from the said Harpers at one half their original cost, de-
ducting a fair valuation of the wear and tear they may
their use, or any injury from other causes.
se. this contract shall cease and deter
that the said Harpers shall have the
f any copies of said work remaining on
such purchase, they paying upon the
s as herein provided.
is distinctly understood that this agree-
the publication of the said work in the
said Herman Melville reserving to
ght to publish the same, or to dispose
publishing the same, in Great Britain
nation.
er & Brothers agree to advance to the
e first day of December, 1848, the
d dollars, on account of this agree-
November 15th., 1848
Herman Melville
Harper & Brothers
Herman Melville
for
"My First Voyage," &c
"Redburn"
Copied
H. Melville,
Apl 28/49
"Typee"
Copied
Agreement
Between
Harper & Brothers
and
Herman Melville
Feby 20th 1852.
Pierre
Copied
Agreement
Between
Harper and Brothers
and
Herman Melville
Sept 12 1851.
The Whale.
Moby Dick
To be kept by
H & B
Copied

42. Dante Gabriel Rossetti, 1828–1882. Tennyson reading "Maud." Ink and sepia wash drawing, inscribed in Rossetti's hand "I hate the dreadful hollow behind the little wood." [London, 27 September 1855] 18.5 x 12 cm.

Tennyson read his poem "Maud" at a party given by Elizabeth Barrett and Robert Browning. Rossetti presented the drawing to Robert Browning, and ultimately the noted collector A. E. Newton mounted it in an album together with a note from Robert Browning identifying the occasion and with a letter from Mrs. Browning to Mrs. Theodore Martin in which she describes Tennyson's performance.

GIFT OF THE VISCOUNTESS ECCLES (PH.D, 1949), 1977

Executive Mansion
June 26. 1861

My Dear Sir,

It is with feelings of deep gratitude not unmingled with diffidence, that I accept the honor which the Trustees of Columbia College have through you, conferred upon me.

It gives me the greatest pleasure to receive from a source so universally respected, such a manifestation of confidence and good will. I accept it less as a personal courtesy than as a grateful indication of the spirit which animates all classes of our people, to preserve inviolate the institutions to whose fostering protection we owe all the progress we have made, as well in material and political advancement as in the higher fields of literature and science.

Your Obt. Servt.
A. Lincoln

Hon Charles King
&c &c

43

43. Abraham Lincoln, 1809–1865. Autograph letter, signed, to Charles King. Washington, D.C., 26 June 1861.

To the president of Columbia University, the letter, in the hand of John Hay, was written on the day that Lincoln received an honorary degree from the university, six months after the secession of South Carolina and scarcely two months before the firing on Fort Sumter. The letter emphasizes Lincoln's gratitude for the "manifestation of confidence and good will" the degree represented, coming "from a source so universally respected."

GIFT OF JANET HALDANE AND FAMILY IN MEMORY OF DR. A.R.B. HALDANE, 1983

44. Anthony Trollope, 1815–1882. *Sir Harry Hotspur of Humblethwaite.* London: Hust and Blackett, 1871.

First edition, first issue. Inscribed to George Eliot, "To the first living English novelist from her most affectionate friend The author." From the library of Carroll A. Wilson with his bookplate and with the sales label of the 1923 Lewes sale.

GIFT OF ELEANOR M. TILTON (PH.D., 1947), 1983

45. Randolph Caldecott, 1846–1886. "Xmas eve; introduction to the hall." Watercolor and wash drawing for the story "Christmas Eve," published in *Old Christmas: From the Sketch book of Washington Irving* (London: Macmillan, 1875), 1874. 17 x 12 cm.

Caldecott's first notable book illustrations, their success leading to his being chosen by publisher Edmund Evans as Walter Crane's successor; the entire suite of 112 drawings is present in the collection.

PURCHASED ON THE FRIENDS ENDOWED FUND, 1983

46. *Naughty girl's and boy's magic transformations*. New York: McLouglin Brothers, [ca. 1880].

One of over 800 children's books published in color by McLoughlin Brothers, a major New York publisher of illustrated books for young people in the nineteenth century, which were presented by Professor Henne.

GIFT OF FRANCES HENNE, 1979

47. Arthur Conan Doyle, 1859–1930. "J. Habbakuk Jephson's statement." Autograph manuscript, signed, 49 p. Southsea, England, [1883].

First published in *Cornhill Magazine*, January 1884, this story marks the beginning of Doyle's career as an author.

PURCHASED ON THE SOLTON (A.B., 1916) AND JULIA ENGEL FUND, 1976

48. Edward A. MacDowell, 1861–1908. Sketchbook for the "Indian Suite no. 2." Autograph manuscript, 69 p. [1891–92].

Tiffany silver cup presented to MacDowell by his students, May 14, 1904. 13 cm.

A Columbia University committee, after hearing a performance of this work by the Boston Symphony Orchestra on January 23, 1896, decided to recommend MacDowell to become the university's first professor of music. The cup is engraved with the names of his students and inscribed, "with the high esteem and affection of his classes at Columbia University. . . ."

GIFT OF THE MARY FLAGLER CARY CHARITABLE TRUST, 1969 (MANUSCRIPT) AND MR. AND MRS. ROBERT E. EVANS, 1972 (CUP)

49. T. J. Cobden-Sanderson, 1840–1922. Binding on *Thoughts of the Emperor Marcus Aurelius* (London, 1890). Doves bindery, 1893.

Tan morocco, gilt, brocade doublures; a binding produced by Cobden-Sanderson during the first year of the Doves bindery, seven years before the founding of the Doves Press.

GIFT OF MESSRS. ADRIAN P. AND DAVID E. MOORE FROM THE ESTATE OF EDITH PULITZER MOORE, 1975

Indian Suite. last movement
Score page 116. commence this
at 10th measure.

50. John Keats, 1795–1821. *The eve of St. Agnes.* [River Forest, Illinois]: Printed at the Auvergne Press by William H. Winslow and Chauncey L. Williams, 1896.

Number 47 of 65 numbered copies, the title page was designed by Frank Lloyd Wright. Inscribed by Winslow; from the library of Frances Steloff with her bookplate.

GIFT OF JAMES L. WEIL IN HONOR OF JACK STILLINGER, 1990

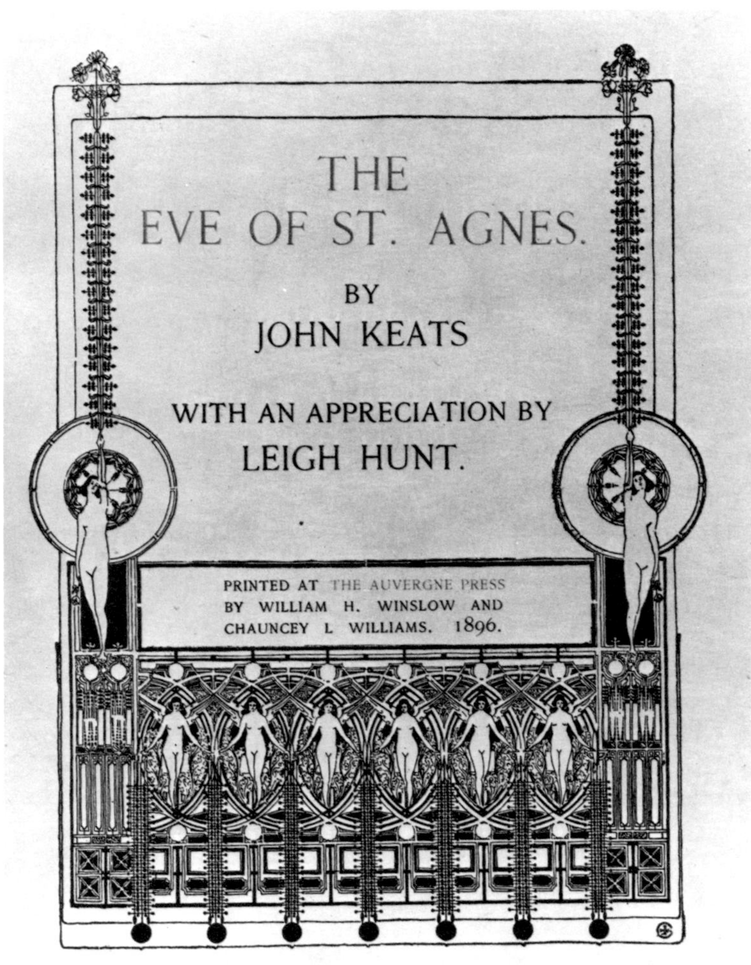

51. Stephen Crane, 1871–1900. Autograph letter, signed, to William H. Crane. Athens, Greece, 10 April [1897].

Crane begins his letter to his brother "I arrived in Athens three days ago and am going to the frontier shortly. I expect to get a position on the staff of the Crown Prince. Won't that be great?" Crane had gone to Greece to cover the Greco-Turkish War, a war that lasted only a month, and with no field experience he was naive in expecting an appointment.

PURCHASED ON THE SOLTON (A.B., 1916) AND JULIA ENGEL FUND, 1974

52. Oliver Wendell Holmes, Jr., 1841–1935. Autograph letter, signed, to P. E. Mason. Boston, 1 March 1899.

Written at the time Holmes became Chief Justice of Massachusetts, he advises an aspiring lawyer on his education, recommending books for study and giving counsel on the practice of law.

GIFT OF STUART B. SCHIMMEL, 1985

53. Henry Murger, 1840–1861. *Scènes de la vie de bohème*. Paris: Librarie de la Collection des Dix, 1902.

Illustrated by Charles Léandre with color wood engravings by Eugène Decisy. Number 29 of 35 exemplars on *Japon blanc*, with two states of all of the illustrations and with decompositions of one plate.

GIFT OF GORDON N. RAY (LL.D., 1969), 1976

54. Persius and Juvenal. *Satiurae*. Oxford: Clarendon Press, 1903.

Two copies from the library of A. E. Housman, annotated extensively by him while preparing his edition of Juvenal for publication by Grant Richards in 1905.

GIFT OF GILBERT HIGHET, 1976

55. Frank Norris, 1870–1902. "A lost story." Autograph manuscript, signed, 19 leaves.

Presumably the printer's copy for the *Century Magazine*, July 1903, appearance; profusely annotated with corrections, deletions, and insertions.

PURCHASED ON THE SOLTON (A.B., 1916) AND JULIA ENGEL FUND, 1978

56. *Le festin d'Esope. Revue des belles lettres.* No. 1, Novembre 1903. Paris.

Friend of Picasso and Braque, the poet Apollinaire founded and edited this journal which lasted for nine issues from November 1903 to August 1904. This first issue is inscribed by Apollinaire on the front cover to author and editor Henri-Martin Barzun, whose papers contain nearly 7,000 letters and manuscripts of French and American authors.

GIFT OF JACQUES BARZUN (A.B., 1927; A.M., 1928; PH.D., 1932), 1976

57. Edith Wharton, 1862–1937. *The fruit of the tree.* New York: Scribner's sons, 1907.

Stamped on the front paste-down, "Advance Dummy Sample Publication Day, About" and written in pencil, "Oct. 12."

GIFT OF IOLA HAVERSTICK (A.B., 1946, B.; A.M., 1965), 1992

58. Sigmund Freud, 1856–1939. "3 Zeiten." Autograph manuscript, 4 p., St. Annes and n.p., 1 and 8 September 1908.

Notes on Otto Rank's unpublished articles on *Die Nibelungenlied* and on Macaulay, Kleist, Shakespeare, Homer, among other authors.

GIFT OF THE OTTO RANK ASSOCIATION, 1984

59. Max Beerbohm, 1872–1956. "The Fabian Society." Pencil drawing, signed, depicting George Bernard Shaw lecturing to the Society. October 1911. 40.5 x 32 cm.

Beerbohm drew more than forty caricatures of his friend Shaw from 1896 to 1931. Fellow Fabians may be seen seated on the platform behind Shaw, who was an early member of the socialist society and was on its executive committee from 1884 to 1911.

GIFT OF MRS. M. LINCOLN SCHUSTER, 1973

60. Carnegie Corporation of New York. Documents relating to the incorporation and foundation of the Carnegie Corporation. 1911.

Among the documents are the *Act to incorporate Carnegie Corporation of New York*. [Albany, New York], 1911, endorsed on verso; the call to the incorporators of the Corporation for the first meeting, signed by the Andrew Carnegie, Robert A. Franks, James Bertram, Elihu Root, and Henry S. Pritchett; and the draft of the statement of appreciation for Carnegie's gift.

GIFT OF THE CARNEGIE CORPORATION OF NEW YORK, 1990

61. William Rothenstein, 1872–1945. "William Butler Yeats." Black crayon on oatmeal paper, signed, 1914. 22.5 x 17.5 cm.

PURCHASED ON THE ALBERT ULMANN FUND PRESENTED BY RUTH ULMANN SAMUEL, 1985

62. Jessie Tarbox Beals, 1870–1942. Slum children. [New York: 1916]

Lewis W. Hine, 1874–1940. Boys on a tenement stair. ca. 1910.

Photographs documenting tenement and family life from an extensive collection of nearly 7,000 early twentieth-century photographs in the Community Service Society Papers.

GIFT OF THE COMMUNITY SERVICE SOCIETY, 1979

63. Wilfred Owen, 1893–1918. "Spring Offensive" and "The Blind." Autograph manuscripts, 4 p. [Amiens, ca. Sept. 1918].

Six weeks before his death at the front, Owen enclosed these manuscripts in a letter, dated September 22, 1918, to Siegfried Sassoon, who pencilled the notes at the top of the manuscripts and changed the title of "The Blind" to "The Sentry" when it was published.

PURCHASED ON VARIOUS FUNDS, 1979

64. John Masefield, 1878–1967. *Reynard the fox; or, The Ghost Heath run.* London: William Heinemann, 1919.

Number 1 of 250 signed copies printed on English hand-made paper. Inscribed on the fly-leaf to his wife "For Con from Jan. The first copy made of this edition." Masefield embellished this copy for his wife with watercolor and pen and ink drawings on 103 pages.

GIFT OF CORLISS LAMONT (PH.D., 1932), 1977

REYNARD THE FOX

"Hark Hollar, Hark Hollar!" then Robin made
Pip go crash through the cut and laid.
Hounds were over and on his line
With a head like bees upon Tipple Tine.
The sound of the nearness sent a flood
Of terror of death through the fox's blood.
He upped his brush and he cocked his nose,
And he went upwind as a racer goes.

* * * *

Bold Robin Dawe was over first,
Cheering his hounds on at the burst;
The field were spurring to be in it.
"Hold hard, sirs, give them half a minute,"
Came from Sir Peter on his white.
The hounds went romping with delight
Over the grass and got together,
The tail hounds galloped hell-for-leather
After the pack at Myngs's yell.
A cry like every kind of bell
Rang from these rompers as they raced.

* * * *

The riders, thrusting to be placed,
Jammed down their hats and shook their horses;
The hounds romped past with all their forces,
They crashed into the blackthorn e.
The scent was heavy on their sens

73

64

65. Harold Miller Lewis, 1893–1978. Laboratory notebook. Autograph manuscript, signed, 137 p. Paris, 21 July 1918–8 January 1919.

Lewis worked for Edwin H. Armstrong in the Paris laboratory of the U.S. Army Signal Corps. On August 13, 1918, Captain Armstrong described to Corporal Lewis his invention of the superheterodyne circuit and gave him directions for making the first working model, information Lewis recorded in this notebook. The superheterodyne reciever is Armstrong's most far-reaching invention, the basis for most radio, television, and radar receivers.

GIFT OF PENNIE & EDMONDS, 1983

66. David Herbert Lawrence, 1885–1930. "The Sea and Sardinia." Typed manuscript, 305 p., with corrections in the author's hand. [Taormina, ca. March 23, 1921].

The setting copy for the first American edition published by Thomas Seltzer, December 1921.

GIFT OF MRS. ALFRED M. HELLMAN, 1968.

67. Aaron Copland, 1900–1990. "Four motets." Autograph manuscript, signed, 13 p. [Paris, Fall 1921].

Among Copland's earliest compositions, these four works, *a cappella* choral settings of Biblical verses, were composed while he was a student of Nadia Boulanger; they were first conducted by Boulanger in Paris in 1924.

GIFT OF JACK BEESON, 1984

68. Arthur Rackham, 1867–1939. Goldfish. Pen and ink and watercolor drawing, signed. [ca. 1922–1925]. 28 x 24 cm.

The painting was done as part of a series of magazine illustrations advertising Colgate's Cashmere Bouquet soap.

GIFT OF MICHAEL A. LOEB (A.B., 1950), 1991

69. Gertrude Stein, 1874–1946. *A book concluding with as a wife has a cow, a love story*. Paris, La Galerie Simon, 1926.

Illustrated with lithographs by Juan Gris. Number 51 of 112 copies signed by the author and illustrator.

PURCHASED ON THE SOLTON (A.B., 1916) AND JULIA ENGEL FUND, 1971

69

70. Joseph Urban, 1872–1933. "Show Boat. Act I scene 1 & 8." Watercolor drawing. [Yonkers? ca. 1927]. 12.5 x 19.5 cm.

One of seven drawings done for the 1927 premiere production of *Show Boat*, the operetta by Edna Ferber and Jerome Kern.

GIFT OF GRETL URBAN, 1987

71. Voltaire, 1694–1778. *Candide*. New York: Random House, 1928.

The first book published with the Random House imprint. Copy P1 of six special hand-colored presentation copies, with an original watercolor drawing by Rockwell Kent, the illustrator of the volume; inscribed to the printer, Elmer Adler, by Kent, the publisher Bennett Cerf, and others associated with the book's production. On the colophon page appears Kent's drawing of a house that became the company's logo.

GIFT OF JOHN M. CRAWFORD, JR., 1975

SHOW · BOAT ·
· ACT · I · Scene 1+8 ·
MOLLIE ABLE

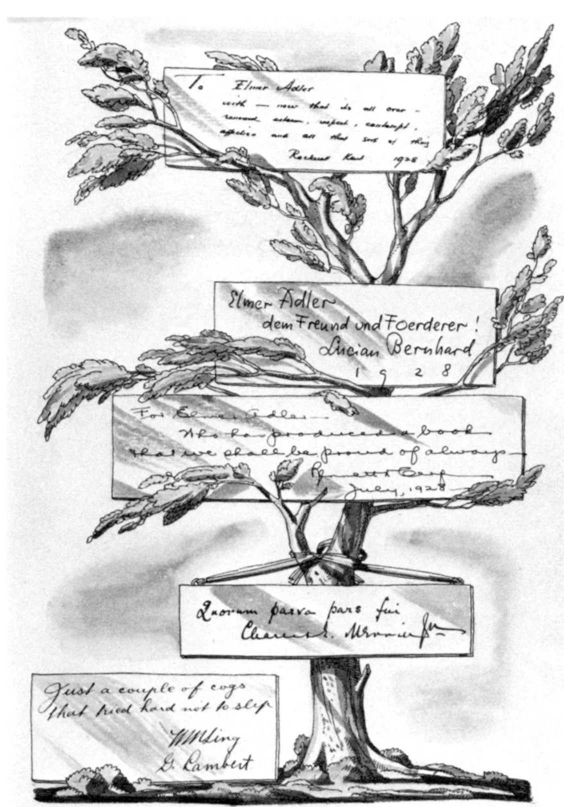
To Elmer Adler
affection and all that sort of thing
1928
Elmer Adler
dem Freund und Foerderer!
Lucian Bernhard
1 9 2 8
For Elmer Adler
who has produced a book
that we shall be proud of always
July, 1928
Quorum parva pars fui
Just a couple of cogs
that tried hard not to slip
G. Lambert

72. Eugene O'Neill, 1888–1953. Forewords to his collected plays. Typed manuscript, 27 p. [Sea Island, Georgia, May–June 1934].

Originally written by Saxe Commins for Scribner's edition of O'Neill's *Plays* (New York, 1934–1935), the manuscript has been extensively corrected in pencil by the playwright.

GIFT OF RANDOM HOUSE, COURTESY OF BENNETT CERF (A.B., 1920) AND DONALD S. KLOPFER, 1970

73. Jean Cocteau, 1889–1963. *Mythologie*. Paris: 4 Chemins, 1934.

Number 30 of 110 copies. With ten original signed lithographs by Giorgio de Chirico.

GIFT OF FRANCIS STEEGMULLER (A.B., 1927; A.M., 1928), 1979

74. James Joyce, 1882–1941. *Ulysses*. New York: Random House, 1934.

Salesman's dummy for the first American edition.

GIFT OF RONALD L. DZIERBICKI IN MEMORY OF MARGUERITE A. COHN, 1990

75. Henri Matisse, 1869–1954. Engraved steel plate for the illustration of the Polyphemus episode in James Joyce's *Ulysses* (New York: Limited Editions Club, 1935). 26.5 x 21 cm.

Matisse illustrated *Ulysses* with six engravings; other plates in the series, present in the collection, depict the "Circe," "Ithaca," and "Calypso" episodes.

GIFT OF HELEN MACY, 1976

76. Bette Davis, 1908–1989. Portrait photograph by Elmer Fryer.

Inscribed to W. Seward, Jr. One of a collection of 1,300 movies stills, many inscribed, from the silent screen era to the present.

GIFT OF PAUL R. PALMER (M.S., 1950; A.M., 1955), 1991

77. John Steinbeck, 1902–1968. Of mice and men. Autograph manuscript, signed, 13 p. in notebook. [New York? 1937?].

Drafts of additions to the script of the screen play.

GIFT OF ANNIE LAURIE WILLIAMS, 1971

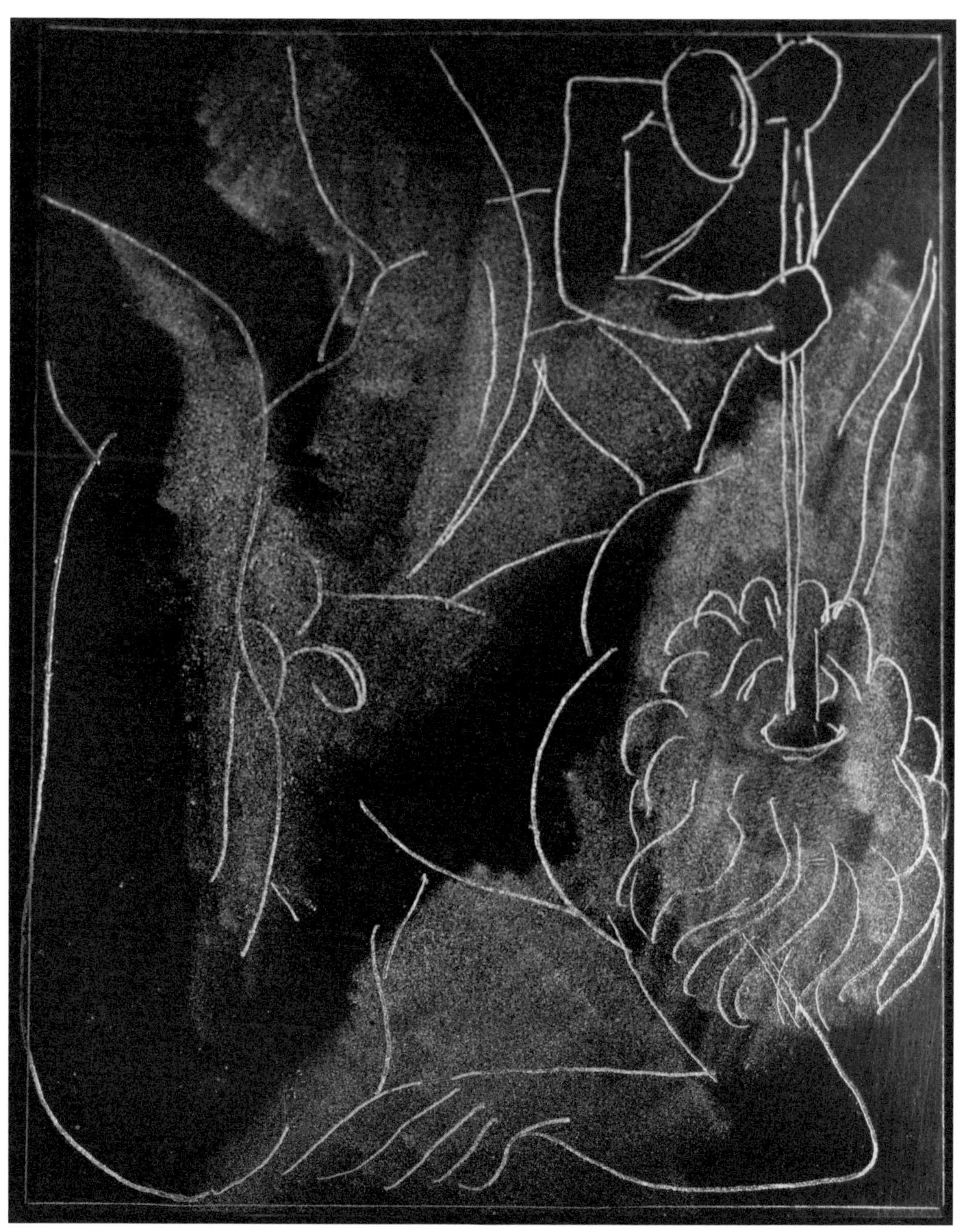

78. Rockwell Kent, 1882–1971. Egg cup and dessert plate from the "Moby Dick" ceramic dinnerware set. Vernon Kilns, Los Angeles, 1938.

Two of twelve pieces. Kent produced three patterns for dinnerware manufactured between 1938 and 1940; the "Moby Dick" pattern uses designs of whaling ships and whales different from the Kent drawings in the famous edition of the Melville novel published in 1930.

GIFT OF SALLY KENT, 1973

78

79. P. G. Wodehouse, 1881-1975. Autograph postcards, signed, to Paul Revere Reynolds. [Tost, Germany] 21 October and 1 November 1940.

Written while a detainee in a prisoner of war camp, Wodehouse writes his literary agent, "Am quite happy here and have thought out new novel. Am hoping be able write it. When I was interned, I had finished a Jeeves novel. All but four chapters, also two short stories."

GIFT OF ROBBIN REYNOLDS, 1988

80. Tammaro de Marinis, 1878–1969. *Il castello di Monselice: Raccolta degli antichi veneziani figurati.* Verona: Dai torchi della Officina Bodoni, 1941.

The author's copy of his catalog of the monumental private library of fifteenth- and sixteenth-century Venetian illustrated books, formerly in the library of Prince D'Essling. The work, illustrated with ninety-two full-page photogravures, was printed during the war in an edition of 310 copies and distributed to personal friends by Conte Vittori Cini, the owner of Monselice; bound by Gruel of Paris in full morocco, richly blind-stamped in the fifteenth-century Venetian style.

PURCHASED WITH FUNDS DONATED BY JULIA P. WIGHTMAN THROUGH THE CALEB C. AND JULIA W. DULA FOUNDATION, 1986

81. Ellery Queen. "The Roman hat mystery."

Typed manuscript, signed, with handwritten corrections and additions, 292 pages (carbon).

The Roman hat mystery. New York: Frederick A. Stokes Company, 1929.

107.

Piggott, who had disappeared into a small kitchen, returned staggering under the burden of a half-empty case of liquor-bottles.

Ellery and his father bent over the case. The Inspector removed a cork gingerly, sniffed the contents, then handed the bottle to Piggott, who followed his superior's example critically.

"Looks and smells okay," said the detective. "But I'd hate to take a chance tasting this stuff---after last night."

"You're perfectly justified in your caution," chuckled Ellery. "But if you should change your mind and decide to invoke the spirit of Bacchus, Piggott, let me suggest this prayer: O Wine, if thou hast no name to be known by, let us call thee Death!"*

"I'll have the firewater analyzed," growled Queen. "Scotch and rye mixed, and the labels look like the real thing. But then you never can tell. . . ." Ellery suddenly grasped his father's arm, leaning forward tensely. The three men stiffened.

A barely audible scratching came to their ears, proceeding from the foyer.

"Sounds as if somebody is using a key on the door," whispered Queen. "Duck out, Piggott---jump whoever it is as soon as he gets inside!"

Piggott darted through the living-room into the foyer. Queen and Ellery waited in the bedroom, concealed from view.

There was utter silence now except for the scraping on the outer door. The newcomer seemed to be having difficulty with the key. Suddenly the rasp of the lock-tumblers falling back was heard and an instant later the door swung open. It slammed shut almost immediately.

A muffled cry, a hoarse bull-like voice, Piggott's half-strangled oath, the frenzied shuffling of feet---and Ellery and his father were speeding across the living-room to the foyer.

Piggott was struggling in the arms of a burly, powerful man dressed in black. A suit-case lay on the floor to one side, as if it had been thrown there during the tussle. A newspaper was fluttering through the air, settling on the parquet just as Ellery reached the cursing men.

*Ellery Queen was here probably paraphrasing the [illegible] quotation from Shakespeare: "O thou invisible spirit of wine, if thou hast no name to be known by, let us call thee devil."

The manuscript of the first of the mysteries written by Manfred Lee, 1905–1871, and Frederick Dannay, 1905–1982, under the pseudonym, Ellery Queen, is inscribed: "This is the only carbon-copy of the original typescript of 'The Roman Hat Mystery' still in existence. The original typescript, and all other carbon-copies, were destroyed. 'Ellery Queen' 12/22/41." The first edition is inscribed by Lee to his family, "August 19, 1929 To the Folks With much Love . . . Manny."

GIFT OF RICHARD AND DOUGLAS DANNAY, 1987 (MANUSCRIPT) AND PATRICIA LEE CALDWELL, 1990 (BOOK)

82. William Faulkner, 1892–1962. *Go down, Moses and other stories.* New York: Random House, 1942.

First printing. Copy number 1 of 100 copies, signed. Gifts from Phyllis Cerf Wagner and the Cerf Foundation include eight copies of Faulkner limited first editions which are designated "Copy 1" and five copies designated "Copy 2."

GIFT OF THE PHYLLIS AND BENNETT CERF (A.B., 1920) FOUNDATION, 1975

83. Cornell Woolrich, 1903–1968. "Night has a thousand eyes." Typed manuscript with holograph corrections, 372 p. [New York, ca. 1945].

Night has a thousand eyes. New York: Farrar & Rinehart, 1945.

Woolrich published eleven novels during the 1940s, four using the pseudonym William Irish, and one, George Hopley, for the publication of this novel of terrror.

BEQUEST OF CORNELL WOOLRICH (COLLEGE CLASS OF 1925), 1971 (MANUSCRIPT) AND GIFT OF MR. AND MRS. STANLEY WERTHEIM, 1988 (BOOK)

84. George Santayana, 1863–1952. "Persons and places: the background of my life. Volume second." Autograph manuscript, signed, 241 p. [Rome, 1944].

Published with the subtitle *The middle years* (New York, Charles Scribner's sons, 1945), this is one portion of the entire holograph manuscript of the autobiography in the Santayana papers.

GIFT OF CORLISS LAMONT (PH.D., 1932), 1983

85

85. André Gide, 1869–1951. Typed and autograph letter, signed, to Justin O'Brien. Paris, 29 November and 2 December 1948.

Portrait photograph by Laure Albin Guillot. 1945.

Gide writes in his letter about O'Brien's *Maxims of Marcel Proust* (New York: Columbia University Press, 1948) and gives his evaluation of Proust as a writer. The photograph is inscribed "á Justin O'Brien au toute sympathie juillet 1946 André Gide."

GIFT OF MRS. JUSTIN O'BRIEN, 1969 AND 1983

86. Robert Lowell, 1917–1977. *Lord Weary's castle*. New York: Harcourt, Brace, 1946.

First edition with extensive corrections and additions throughout by Lowell. Inscribed to William Direski, "For Bill, for his collection, his sanity, his lovely first book—love Cal, Robert Lowell."

PURCHASED ON THE AARON W. BERG (A.B., 1924; LL.B., 1927) FUND, 1981

87. Sir Winston Churchill, 1874–1965. Autograph letter, signed, to Daniel Longwell. Marrakech, 5 January 1948.

The second world war; The gathering storm. Boston: Houghton Mifflin Company, 1948.

As is apparent from Churchill's letter, Longwell was closely involved in the editing of Churchill's history of World War II, serialized in *Life* magazine of which Longwell was a founding editor and chairman of the board of editors, 1946–1954. The copy of the first volume of the published history is inscribed by Churchill to his editor.

GIFT OF MRS. DANIEL LONGWELL, 1969

88. Dorothy Richardson, 1873–1957. Autograph letter, signed, to Lita Rothbard (Hornick) with Lita Hornick's notes. Cornwall, England, 20 December 1948.

Richardson, whose *Pilgrimage* novels are often cited as the first instances of stream of consciousness writing, replied to a query from Lita Hornick who was then working on her master's degree, "Of Freud, Jung & Co., of Proust, James Joyce & Virginia Woolf . . . I knew nothing until after *Pilgrimage* was well-advanced."

GIFT OF LITA HORNICK (A.B., 1948 B; A.M., 1949; PH.D., 1958), 1990

89. Thomas Merton, 1915–1968. "The seven storey mountain." Typed manuscript, 649 p., with Merton's emendations in ink. [Trappist, Kentucky, 1948].

The original setting-copy for the first edition, the manuscript also has editor Robert Giroux's corrections in pencil and a copy editor's markings in red pencil.

GIFT OF ROBERT GIROUX (A.B., 1936), 1991

90. Cole Porter, 1893–1964, and Bella Spewack, 1899–1990. *Kiss me, Kate.* New York: Salem Corporation, [1947 or 1948]. Mimeograph playscript with manuscript revisions.

Photograph of Cole Porter and Bella Spewack at the rehearsal of *Kiss me, Kate*, October 1948.

Antoinette Perry ["Tony"] Award. 1949.

The medal was presented by The American Theatre Wing to Sam and Bella Spewack for *Kiss me, Kate.*

GIFT OF THE ESTATE OF BELLA SPEWACK, 1990

91. Edith Sitwell, 1887–1965. "Some notes on my own poetry." Typed manuscript with autograph corrections and emendations, 47 p. ca. 1949.

Sitwell confirms the sincerity and care which have gone into her poetry in this long introduction to her *The canticle of the rose: poems, 1917-1949* (New York: Vanguard Press, 1949).

GIFT OF EVELYN SHRIFTE, 1991

92. Jack Kerouac, 1922–1969. "Mexico City blues." Typed manuscript, signed. 1955.

Mexico City blues (242 choruses). New York: Grove Press, 1959.

The book is inscribed by the author to Allen Ginsberg with three pen and ink drawings. Kerouac typed the manuscript on two rolls of paper which total nearly 12½ feet.

PURCHASED ON VARIOUS FUNDS, 1975

93. John Fitzgerald Kennedy, 1917–1963. Typed letter, signed, to Allan Nevins. Washington, D.C., 6 July 1955.

Kennedy thanks Nevins for agreeing to write the preface to *Profiles in courage* (New York: Harper & Row, 1956) and requests Nevins's "frank criticism, comments and suggestions, however major or however petty—not only on the historical accuracy of these chapters, but also on the general theme, style, interest and overall contribution."

BEQUEST OF ALLAN NEVINS (HON.LITT.D., 1960), 1971

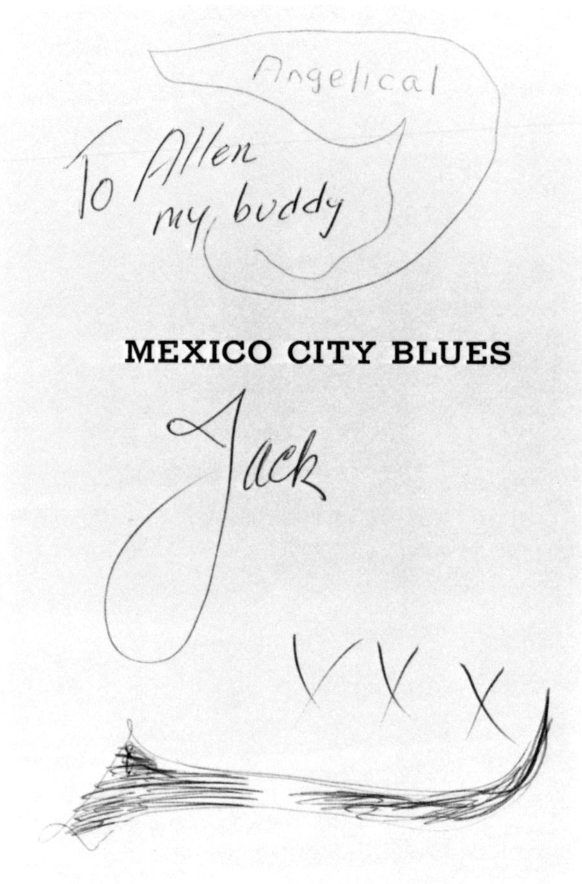

92

94. Allen Ginsberg, 1926– . "Howl for Carl Solomon." Typed manuscript with revisions and corrections in the author's hand, 7 p. [Berkeley, California, January, 1956].

Howl for Carl Solomon. Mimeograph. [San Francisco: 1956].

This copy was sent to Ginsberg's former English professor at Columbia Mark Van Doren.

GIFT OF MARK VAN DOREN (PH.D., 1921), 1967 (MIMEOGRAPH) AND PURCHASED ON VARIOUS FUNDS, 1974 (MANUSCRIPT)

95. Virgil Thomson, 1896–1989. "Virgil Thomson." Autograph manuscript, 1,231 p. ca. 1965.

The Thomson papers contain, in addition, the outlines, notes, typescripts, galleys, and production materials for the composer and critic's autobiography, first published by Alfred Knopf in 1966.

GIFT OF VIRGIL THOMSON (HON.MUS.D., 1978), 1981

96. John Fitzgerald Kennedy, 1917–1963. Typed letter, signed, to Whitney M. Young, Jr. Washington, D.C., 27 November 1962; with pen used in signing ceremony.

Kennedy had criticized President Eisenhower during the election campaign for not eliminating discrimination in housing "by the stroke of a pen." On November 20, Kennedy issued an executive order prohibiting racial and religious discrimination in housing built or purchased with Federal aid and set up the President's Committee on Equal Opportunity in Housing.

GIFT OF MRS. MARGARET YOUNG IN MEMORY OF WHITNEY M. YOUNG, JR. (LL.D., 1971), 1975

97. Marianne Moore, 1887–1972. *The absentee.* New York: House of Books, 1962. (Number 14 of the Crown Octavos).

Copy number 1, inscribed to Marguerite A. Cohn, proprietor of House of Books, "Marianne Moore is a grateful author, Marguerite (Author? part-author) and whole beneficiary, of a big hearted publisher May 17, 1962."

GIFT OF CAROL Z. ROTHKOPF (A.M., 1952) IN MEMORY OF MARGUERITE A. COHN, 1984

98. Fidel Castro, 1926– . Interview conducted by Lee Lockwood at Isle of Pines, Cuba. Typed manuscript, signed and dated by Castro, 17 May 1966, with manuscript corrections throughout, 259 p.

The interview was conducted for Lockwood's book *Castro's Cuba, Cuba's Fidel* (New York: Macmillan, 1967).

GIFT OF LEE LOCKWOOD, 1967

THIS FIRST EDITION IS LIMITED TO
THREE HUNDRED NUMBERED COPIES
SIGNED BY THE AUTHOR
THIS IS NO. 1

Marianne Moore
is a grateful author,
Marguerite
(author? part-author)
and whole beneficiary, of a big-hearted
publisher
May 17, 1962

Humming-bird

I can imagine in some otherworld
Primeval-dumb, far-back
In that most awful stillness, that only gasped and hummed
Humming-birds raced down the avenues

Before anything had a soul
While life was a heave of Matter half inanimate
This little bit chipped off in brilliance
And went whizzing through the slow vast succulent stems

I believe there were no flowers then
In the world where humming=bird flashed ahead of creation
I believe he pierced the slow vegetable veins with his long beak

Probably he was big
As mosses and little lizards they say were once big
Probably he was a jabbing terrifying monster

We look at him through the wrong end of the long
telescope of time
Luckily for us

D.H. Lawrence: Espanola

99. Saul Steinberg, 1914– . The labyrinth. Pen and ink drawing, signed, 1967, for an illustration published in Paul Tillich's *My search for absolutes* (New York: Simon & Schuster, 1967). 46.5 x 32 cm.

Inscribed by the artist, "For Nanda [Ruth Nanda Anshen] with affection." One of 17 drawings created for the volume that was part of the Credo Perspectives series, founded and edited by Dr. Anshen.

GIFT OF RUTH NANDA ANSHEN, 1988

100. Margaret Adams. 1912– . "Humming-bird" from *Birds, beasts and flowers* by D. H. Lawrence. Manuscript on vellum. 1968. 40.5 x 30.5 cm.

The text is written by the English calligrapher Margaret Adams in black and blue ink, the title in burnished gold; the whole is surrounded by a delicate and evocative illumination by C. Harry Adams depicting humming-birds against a background of leaves and vines.

GIFT OF THE FRIENDS OF THE LIBRARIES, 1968

101. Charles Saxon, 1920–1989. Sheep on Wall Street. Pastel drawing. Copyright 1973 by the *New Yorker*. 38 x 28 cm.

Cover design which illustrates the humor and underlying social commentary characteristic of Saxon's cartoons and art work that he produced for national magazines from the 1940s through the 1980s.

GIFT OF NANCY SAXON, 1991

102. Michel Butor, 1926– . *Zodiaque de nuages*. Artist's book. Watercolor, ink and colored pencil, 9 unbound folded leaves issued in paper portfolio, cloth portfolio, and slipcase. [Paris?] 1984.

Butor's holograph manuscript is in silver ink, with illustrations by Julius Baltazar. One of two numbered copies, signed by the author and the illustrator.

PURCHASED ON THE ALBERT ULMANN FUND, PRESENTED BY RUTH ULMANN SAMUEL, 1986

SAXON

102

103. Samuel Beckett, 1906–1989. *Textes pour riens. 13*. Paris: Yves Rivière, 1987.

Number 23 of 75 copies, signed by the author and illustrator. With five lithographs on Japan paper by Bram van Velde, each signed by the artist; printed at the Imprimerie nationale.

GIFT OF SIGHLE KENNEDY (A.M., 1964, PH.D., 1969) IN MEMORY OF WILLIAM YORK TINDALL (A.B., 1925; A.M., 1926; PH.D., 1934), 1990

INDEXES

INDEX OF ENTRIES

Numbers refer to items

INDEX OF DONORS

Numbers refer to items

1,000 copies of this book have been printed in Sabon type on Monadnock Dulcet paper at The Stinehour Press in Lunenburg, Vermont. Designed by Jerry Kelly.